A HUNDRED AND FIFTIETH
ANNIVERSARY ALBUM OF BASEBALL

A Hundred and Fiftieth Anniversary

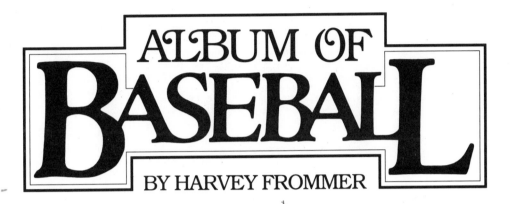

ALBUM OF
BASEBALL

BY HARVEY FROMMER

FRANKLIN WATTS · NEW YORK · LONDON · TORONTO · SYDNEY · 1988

Photographs courtesy of:
Los Angeles Times, Inc.: p. 2; National Baseball Library, Cooperstown, NY: pp. 8, 10, 12, 14, 16 (bottom left, right), 18 (bottom left, right), 19 (top left, bottom), 21, 22, 25, 26 (bottom, Carl Seid), 27, 29 (top, center, bottom right), 30, 31 (top, bottom right), 34 (top), 35, 36, (top left, top right, bottom left), 38, 39 (bottom), 42 (bottom center), 43 (bottom left), 45 (top left), 47 (top left, right), 48, 51 (top right, bottom left), 52, 60 (top), 62 (top, bottom right), 64 (top left, bottom right), 65, 68 (top left, bottom), 69 (bottom), 71 (top left, bottom), 73, 76 (top right), 85 (top left), 86, 88 (bottom left, top right, bottom right); New York Public Library Picture Collection: pp. 13, 16 (top left), 18 (top), 19 (top right); American League: pp. 31 (bottom left), 47 (bottom left), 54 (top); UPI: 34 (bottom left, right), 39 (top left), 40 (top), 51 (top left, bottom), 55 (top left, bottom), 60 (bottom), 64 (top right), 69 (top), 71 (top right), 76 (left), 79; Harvey Frommer Collection: pp. 36 (bottom right), 50, 55 (top right); AP: pp. 29 (bottom left), 39 (top right), 40 (bottom), 51 (bottom right), 63 (bottom); Pittsburgh Pirates: p. 42 (top left, right); San Diego Padres: p. 42 (bottom left); California Angels: pp. 42 (bottom right), 76 (bottom right); Chicago Cubs: pp. 43 (top), 85 (bottom); St. Louis Cardinals: pp. 43 (center, bottom center), 64 (bottom left), 82, 87, 88 (top left); Atlanta Braves: pp. 43 (bottom right), 83 (top left); New York Convention & Visitors Bureau: pp. 44 (top left), 45 (bottom left); New York Yankees: pp. 44 (top left and right, center right), 45 (top right, bottom right), 54 (bottom), 59, 72, 80 (top right), 85 (top right); Los Angeles Dodgers, Inc.: pp. 44 (bottom left, right), 45 (top center), 62 (bottom left), 63 (top), 80 (bottom right); San Francisco Giants: p. 68 (top right); Royal Canadians: p. 80 (top left); Philadelphia Phillies: pp. 80 (bottom left), 83 (bottom); Houston Astros: 83 (top right).

Library of Congress Cataloging in Publication Data

Frommer, Harvey.
A hundred and fiftieth anniversary album of baseball / by Harvey Frommer.
p. cm.—(A Picture album)
Includes index.
Summary: A history of the popular American sport from before the turn of the century to the modern day, discussing its changes under the impact of changing times.
ISBN 0-531-10588-1
1. Baseball—United States—History—Juvenile literature.
2. Baseball—History. I. Title. II. Title 150th album of baseball. III. Series.
GV863.A1F75 1988
796.357′0973—dc19   88-5740 CIP AC

J
796.357
FRO

CONTENTS

A HUNDRED AND FIFTIETH ANNIVERSARY ALBUM OF BASEBALL

Above left: Abner Doubleday
Above right: Alexander J. Cartwright,
the man who gave baseball its
basic structure and rules.
Below: Doubleday Field in Cooperstown,
New York, where legend has it
that the first baseball game was played.

Chapter One

BEGINNINGS

Baseball has been America's game for almost fifteen decades. It is a sport played and watched by millions of people around the world throughout their lives. Baseball is Opening Day and the seventh game of the World Series, the man in blue—the umpire—the seventh-inning stretch, the box score, the program, the statistic. Baseball is the smack of a white ball into the grainy oiled leather of a glove, the crack of the wooden bat, the fixed geometry of the diamond, the sprawling outfield that echoes the wide open spaces of another America.

That other America was the cradle for baseball's beginnings. Legend designates Major General Abner Doubleday of Cooperstown, New York, as the man who laid out the first baseball diamond, in a cow pasture in Cooperstown in 1839. This legend was given some recognition when the Baseball Hall of Fame was established at Cooperstown in baseball's "centennial" year of 1939. Thus, 1989 is generally viewed as baseball's 150th anniversary.

Doubleday may or may not have first thought of the game of baseball, but it was Alexander J. Cartwright who gave the game its basic structure, in 1845. Cartwright's rules included foul lines, nine players to a side, nine innings to a game, and a diamond-shaped infield with bases at each corner located 90 feet (27 m) apart. An inning was called a "hand" and a run an "ace." The style and some of the substance of Cartwright's game were a bit different from the baseball of today, but the foundation of the national pastime was laid.

Baseball's first recorded match was played at the Elysian Fields in Hoboken, New Jersey, on June 19, 1846. The New York Nine lost to Cartwright's New York Knickerbockers, 23–1.

In 1858, the National Association of Baseball Players was organized, making the rules of the sport more uniform. Baseball's

Above: an artist's depiction of an early
baseball match at the Elysian Fields in
Hoboken, New Jersey. *Below:* the Cincinnati Red
Stockings of 1869. Harry Wright, the organizer,
is the third man from the left, standing.

popularity grew throughout the 1850s and 1860s. The sport was even played by soldiers during the Civil War.

The Cincinnati Red Stockings of 1869, organized by Harry Wright, a jeweler and former star cricket player, was baseball's first all-professional team. During the 1869 season the Red Stockings traveled 12,000 miles (19,200 km) and played baseball throughout the Northeast and West. The team won sixty-four games and there was one disputed tie. The following season the Cincinnati streak reached ninety-two straight wins. The fabled success of the Red Stockings ended the days of amateur-only competition and triggered the beginnings of professional baseball.

In 1871, the National Association of Professional Baseball was created. The first professional league was run mainly by the players. Then, in 1876, the National League (NL), run by owners for profit, came into existence, replacing the older group.

For the remainder of the nineteenth century, the National League, striving to be the only game in town, fought off challenges from other leagues. However, in 1903, following some bitter fighting, the National League grudgingly granted major league status to Ban Johnson's American League (AL) of Professional Baseball Clubs. Baseball now evolved into an organization of two equal leagues—the National League and the American League. The sport stood on the doorstep of the modern age.

The early days of the sport could boast a rich history of outstanding performers: Dan Brouthers, first player to win back-to-back batting titles; Ed Delahanty, second player to hit four home runs in one game; Candy Cummings, perfecter of the curve ball; Hugh Duffy, whose .438 batting average in 1894 is still the highest in baseball history; Wee Willie Keeler, whose record of hitting safely in forty-four straight games stood for as many years; Cy Young, who recorded 511 pitching victories—the most in baseball history; and so on.

Outstanding teams included the Chicago White Stockings, winners of the first pennant in NL history and six pennants in the first eleven years of the league's existence; the Baltimore Orioles of the 1890s, winners of three straight pennants during that decade, who played the hit and run game that would become popular in the next century; and the Boston Red Sox, with eight pennants in the first twenty-five years of the National League.

Above: Dan Brouthers (left)
and Wee Willie Keeler.
Below: Cy Young. *Facing page, above:*
Cap Anson (standing behind young
Clarence Duval, the team "mascot")
and his 1888 Chicago White Sox.
Below: the 1896 Baltimore Orioles

the 1903
Boston Red Sox

Chapter Two

THE MODERN ERA
(1901–1920)

The years 1901 to 1920 are known as the Modern Era of baseball. Various teams rotated as AL pennant winners in that time, while the National League had three teams that formed dynasties: the Pittsburgh Pirates, the New York Giants, and the Chicago Cubs.

The World Series began in 1903, when the AL Boston Red Sox (then called the Pilgrims) and the NL Pittsburgh Pirates met in postseason play to determine a "world" championship team. Boston won that first competition, a best-of-nine-games format. There was no series in 1904, but in 1905 play resumed, and the October Classic has remained to this day one of the highlights of sports in the United States.

The Pirates, led by shortstop Honus Wagner, won the first three NL pennants of the twentieth century and added another flag in 1909. Wagner, a strong-armed, fleet-footed athlete, batted .381 in 1900, his first year with Pittsburgh, to win the first of his eight batting titles. The man they called the "Flying Dutchman" led the National League five times in stolen bases. "Deacon" Phillippe and Jack Chesbro paced the outstanding Pittsburgh pitching staff.

However, the Giants of New York, managed by John McGraw, were the premier team of that time, winning pennants in 1904, 1905, 1911 to 1913, and 1917. In 1916, the Giants set a modern record for consecutive victories, winning twenty-six games in a row. Bucknell University graduate Christy Mathewson was one of the team's superstars. A hurler who set batters up with an assortment of pitches, Matty's speciality was his "fadeaway," today referred to as the screwball. "Iron Man" Joe McGinnity was also part of the Giant pitching staff. In 1903, McGinnity set a record by pitching complete games three times and winning both

Above left: Honus Wagner.
Below left: Christy Mathewson.
Above: Joe McGinnity

ends of a doubleheader. Other fabled Giant stars were shortstop Bill Dahlen, who stole 555 bases in his career, and standout catcher Roger Bresnahan. Rube Marquard teamed with Christy Mathewson to pitch the Giants to their three straight pennants (from 1911 to 1913). In that period, the two premier pitchers won 148 games between them. Their catcher was "Chief" Meyers, an American Indian and a graduate of Dartmouth College. Other Giants stars were centerfielder Fred Snodgrass and "Laughing Larry" Doyle, a sure-handed second baseman.

Another outstanding team of the Modern Era in the National League was the Chicago Cubs, winners of the pennant from 1906 to 1908, 1910, and 1918. The 1906 Cubs won a record 116 games, and the following season recorded the first World Series sweep, winning all the games they played against the Detroit Tigers. Frank the "Peerless Leader" Chance was the manager of the Cubs and also their first baseman—a part of the fabled (Joe) Tinker to (Johnny) Evers to Chance infield double play combination. "Three Fingers" Brown, given that nickname because of a childhood accident that mutilated his pitching hand, won twenty or more games six straight seasons for the Cubs. Other top Chicago pitchers included Carl Lundgren, Orval Overall, Jack Pfiester, and Ed Reulbach. The power hitting of Frank "Wildfire" Schulte and the fine catching of Johnny Kling further strengthened the Cubs.

There were no real dynasties in the first twenty years of the American League, as just four teams won the pennant more than one time. The Chicago White Sox won the American League's first pennant, in 1901, blending pitching and speed. Connie Mack's Philadelphia Athletics recorded pennants in 1902 and 1905. The team's first pennant was achieved in part through the superb pitching of left-handed hurlers Eddie Plank and Rube Waddell. Chief Bender was a major contributor to the 1905 pennant. The Athletics also won the AL pennant in 1910, 1911, 1913, and 1914. Connie Mack assembled what was known as the "$100,000 infield" of first baseman Stuffy McInnis, second baseman Eddie Collins, shortstop Jack Barry, and third baseman Frank "Home Run" Baker.

The White Sox won the 1906 pennant with a weak team batting average of .228 but excellent pitching. The combination earned the Chicago White Sox the nickname "Hitless Wonders."

Bottom left: "Chief" Meyers. *Bottom right:* Larry Doyle.
Above: the 1918 Cubs. *Opposite left:* Chief Bender.
Right: Connie Mack and his Philadelphia Athletics
in 1910. *Below:* the Chicago White Sox of 1906.

WORLD'S MARCH CHAMPIONS

CONNIE MACK

PUBLISHED BY
JOSEPH PALLADINO
CAMDEN, N.J.

M. BROWN.   J. PFEISTER   A. HOFMAN   C.G.WILLIAMS   O. OVERALL   E. REULBACH.   J. KLING.
H. GESSLER.   J. TAYLOR.   H. STEINFELDT.   J. McCORMICK.   F. CHANCE.   J. SHECKARD.   P. MORAN.   F. SCHULTE
C. LUNDGREN.   T. WALSH.   J. EVERS.   J. SLAGLE.   J. TINKER.

CHICAGO NATIONAL LEAGUE BALL CLUB 1906

In 1903 and 1904, the Boston Red Sox recorded the first back-to-back AL pennants. The legendary Cy Young won fifty-four games in those two seasons and was helped by his pitching partner Bill Dineen, winner of more than twenty games each year. The Sox were managed by future Hall of Famer Jimmy Collins, who also played third base. Hitting power was supplied by outfielder Buck Freeman. Aided by more great stars, the Red Sox also won pennants in 1912, 1916, and 1918. Their outfield during most of those years—Tris Speaker in centerfield, Duffy Lewis in left, and Harry Hooper in right field—was outstanding. The Red Sox also benefited from top pitching. Smokey Joe Wood won thirty-four games for Boston in 1912; Eddie Shore, Rube Foster, and a very young pitcher named George Herman ("Babe") Ruth contributed a great deal in 1915. The following season Ruth won twenty-three games to set the pace for the splendid Sox pitching staff.

Ruth, the man they would later call the "Sultan of Swat," played the outfield and pitched for the Red Sox in 1918. He was a remarkable hurler and set a record of 29 2/3 scoreless innings pitched in the 1918 World Series. The following season Ruth devoted most of his time to the outfield and blasted a record—twenty-nine home runs. In 1920, the Red Sox traded Ruth to the New York Yankees. The Babe hammered out fifty-four home runs and became baseball's biggest star. His batting feats did much to wipe away the shame of what was known as the "Black Sox" scandal of that time.

The heavily favored Chicago White Sox had lost the 1919 World Series to the underdog Cincinnati Reds. Rumors circulated during the competition that gamblers had influenced White Sox players to lose. Chicago pitcher Eddie Cicotte later admitted that he had taken a $10,000 bribe to throw the series. Seven other White Sox players were also indicted and were barred from baseball for life. The entire affair became known as the "Black Sox" scandal.

Babe Ruth's home run hitting and lively personality helped draw people's attention away from the scandal, and his gigantic presence also acted as a magnet for fans. Whenever there is a discussion of who was the greatest player of all time, the names of George Herman Ruth and Tyrus Raymond Cobb, two totally opposite personalities, are always brought up.

Above: Tris Speaker (left)
and Smokey Joe Wood.
Below: Eddie Cicotte (left)
and Rube Foster.

Above and below right: Ty Cobb.
Below left: Walter Johnson

Ty Cobb, the "Georgia Peach," led the Detroit Tigers to three straight pennants, from 1907 to 1909. American League batting champion for those three years and for six more seasons after that, Cobb was one of the most admired but also one of the most hated players of his time. On the basepaths his flashing spikes and aggressive play intimidated the opposition, and he set records for base stealing that would stand for decades. Cobb also compiled a lifetime batting average of .367, hitting over .300 in twenty-three of the twenty-four seasons he played.

Other players on the Tigers complemented the skill but never approached the fiery verve of Cobb. "Wahoo" Sam Crawford's specialty was hitting triples. He rapped out 312 of them during his career—a record that still stands. "Germany" Schaefer was a flamboyant infielder, and George Mullin was a top-flight pitcher who recorded sixty-six triumphs during those three Tiger pennant-winning years.

Where Babe Ruth personified home run power, and Ty Cobb symbolized speed on the basepaths, Walter Johnson represented power pitching. One of the greatest pitchers of all time, Johnson toiled for the Washington Senators from 1907 to 1927. Possessor of a blazing fast ball, the mild-mannered Johnson pitched a record 113 career shutouts, seven of these hurled in Opening Day starts for the Senators.

As the first two decades of the twentieth century came to an end, the awesome power and exceptional skills of athletes such as Ty Cobb, Walter Johnson, and Babe Ruth would dominate baseball and continue to do so in the years ahead.

Chapter Three

THE GOLDEN TWENTIES

Baseball in the 1920s filled the need of a nation eager for excitement and heroes after the horrors of the recently ended World War I.

Overall, offense ruled the era. The more hits, the more action was provided for fans. Baseball in the 1920s was characterized by dramatic rallies, many runs scored, and lots of action on the basepaths. From 1920 to 1929, 102 major leaguers rapped out two hundred or more hits in a season; only fifteen players had accomplished that feat in the previous decade. During the 1920s, 147 players recorded more than a hundred RBIs in a season as compared to just twenty-seven players in the ten years previous. Six AL teams batted .300 or more collectively during the 1920s. The 1921 Detroit Tigers batted .316, with Harry Heilmann, a four-time batting champ during the decade, leading the way with a .394 average.

All of these offensive fireworks lured fans to the ballparks of even those teams that did not do well in the standings. A case in point was the sixth-place St. Louis Cardinals of 1924. Led by Rogers Hornsby, who won five straight batting titles, the Cardinals fared much better in attendance than their won-lost record deserved.

Other great hitters of that era included George Sisler of the St. Louis Browns, who batted over .400 twice in the decade, and Ty Cobb and Harry Heilmann, who each accomplished that extraordinary feat once.

Although pitching was a big part of the game in that era, the home run became the game's dominant symbol. Sluggers Babe Ruth and Lou Gehrig, contrasting personalities on the New York Yankees, were the idols of baseball fans everywhere. To the delight of fans, Ruth recorded fifty-four homers in 1920, fifty-nine

Above left: Harry Heilmann
Center: George Sisler. *Right and below:* Lou Gehrig.
Facing page: Babe Ruth

in 1921, and then sixty in 1927. From 1926 to 1931, Ruth averaged slightly more than fifty home runs per season. Not just a powerful slugger, Ruth also hit for a very high average. His lifetime batting average of .342 is one of the best in baseball history. In 1927, when Ruth slugged the stunning total of sixty home runs, Lou Gehrig hammered out forty-seven of them. Both men helped boost the 1927 AL record home run total to 439.

New York City became the baseball capital of the world, as the game became more of an urban sport on the major league level. The Brooklyn Dodgers, New York Yankees, and New York Giants drew almost twenty-six million fans during the decade. Both the Giants and Yankees fielded exciting teams; seven years during that decade the World Series was played in New York City. The Polo Grounds, where the Giants played, and Yankee Stadium, which opened in 1923 and was called "The House that Ruth Built," became powerful symbols of the two teams.

The New York Giants won four straight pennants from 1921 to 1924. The New York Yankees won six pennants, from 1921 to 1923 and 1926 to 1928. Feisty John McGraw managed the New York Giants, a team that relied on spirit, balance, and hit-and-run baseball. Frankie Frisch, the "Fordham Flash," was the team's switch-hitting second baseman for most of the decade. A speedy runner, a deft fielder, and a clutch hitter, Frisch teamed with shortstop Dave "Beauty" Bancroft, giving the Giants a splendid double play combination. Right fielder Mel Ott, who came into his own in 1928, and first baseman Bill Terry were other outstanding Giant stars.

The 1927 Yankee team was known as "Murderer's Row." Considered by many the greatest team of all time, the '27 Yankees recorded 110 victories, won the AL pennant by nineteen games, and swept the Pittsburgh Pirates four straight in the World Series. Babe Ruth was the main force on the Yankees, but there were other stars. Five of the players on the 1927 team batted over .300; four of the Yankees drove in more than a hundred runs. Lou Gehrig not only hit forty-seven home runs, he also led the league in RBIs and recorded more than two hundred hits. Bob Meusel and Tony Lazzeri were among the top five players in the stolen bases. The two leaders in ERA were Yankee pitchers, while Wilcy Moore, a rookie hurler, was a nineteen-game winner.

Although the Yankees and the Giants monopolized the sports pages and dominated competition during the so-called Golden

Above: the Brooklyn Dodgers of 1923

Center: the New York Giants of 1923

Below left: Frankie Frisch

Below right: Bill Terry

St. Louis Cardinals 1926 PENNANT WINNERS

Facing page, from top: the 1927 Yankees;

Washington in 1924;

the Pittsburgh Pirates in 1925.

Above: the 1926 St. Louis Cardinals.

Below left: Lefty Grove

Below right: Jimmy Foxx

Age of baseball, other teams also excelled. Washington won two straight pennants (1924 and 1925) and Philadelphia won three flags in a row (1929 to 1931).

Walter Johnson at age thirty-six won twenty-three games for the 1924 Washington team and the following year won twenty games. The "Big Train's" 1924 seventh-game relief appearance against the New York Giants playing in their fourth straight World Series was one of the most dramatic moments in baseball history. Johnson hurled six scoreless innings, clinching his team's triumph over the favored Giants in the Fall Classic. Other Senator stars included outfielders Goose Goslin and Sam Rice. In 1925, Rice batted .350 and Goslin drove in more than a hundred runs. The other pretender to the New York Yankee throne—the star-studded Philadelphia Athletics—featured such future Hall of Famers as pitcher Robert "Lefty" Grove, slugger Jimmy Foxx, Mickey Cochrane, and Al Simmons.

While the American League in the 1920s was a home run league, the National League's style featured more balanced play. No team reflected this more than the 1925 world champion Pittsburgh Pirates. The Bucs as a team managed to hit just seventy-seven home runs. However, led by Kiki Cuyler and Max Carey, they stole 159 bases. In 1927, driven by the Waner brothers, Paul and Lloyd, the Pirates again won the pennant. Pittsburgh batters collectively recorded only fifty-four home runs that 1927 season, a half-dozen less than Babe Ruth. But the Pirates' balanced attack enabled them to tie the Giants for the National League lead in runs scored (807).

The Pirates, but even more so the St. Louis Cardinals, foreshadowed the style of the next decade of baseball. Steady hitting, speed, and spirited play characterized the St. Louis team, winners of the 1926 World Series. In 1928 the Cardinals traded cocky Rogers Hornsby to the Giants for Frankie Frisch. The trade stunned and infuriated St. Louis fans, but Frisch would win them over and add his verve and fire to a collection of players who would bring the team into the next decade and become known as the "Gashouse Gang."

Chapter Four

BASEBALL AND THE GREAT DEPRESSION

The stock market crashed in 1929, and the United States went through a period of hard times. A depressed economy caused millions of people to be unemployed. Baseball had survived the "Black Sox" scandal. It would now struggle to stay alive during the Great Depression, along with the rest of America.

One constant winning franchise during that era was the New York Yankees. Despite undergoing many changes in personnel, the Yankees won five pennants and five World Series. Joe McCarthy became the Yankee manager, replacing Miller Huggins, who had died. Late in the decade Babe Ruth departed, and then Lou Gehrig and Tony Lazzeri retired. In their places were other stars: centerfielder Joe DiMaggio, a new force on the Yankees, Babe Dahlgren, Joe Gordon, and Charlie Keller.

The New York Giants, managed by Bill Terry, also continued to be a dominant team, winning pennants in 1933, 1936, and 1937. Much of the club's power was supplied by Mel Ott, who would record 511 lifetime home runs. The future Hall of Famer with a very unorthodox batting style was the NL home run champion from 1936 to 1938. Left-handed pitcher "King" Carl Hubbell baffled batters with a screwball that he threw at different speeds and blended with a deceptive change of pace. Hubbell won 253 games for the Giants in a sixteen-year career.

The most exciting team of that time played on the banks of the Mississippi—the St. Louis Cardinals. A flamboyant assortment of athletes, the Redbirds won three of the first five NL pennants in the 1930s. Standout Cardinals included Jay Hanna, Dizzy Dean and his brother Paul, Joe Medwick, "Pepper" Martin, and Leo Durocher.

Much of the talent on the team came from their "farm system," a concept invented by shrewd St. Louis general manager

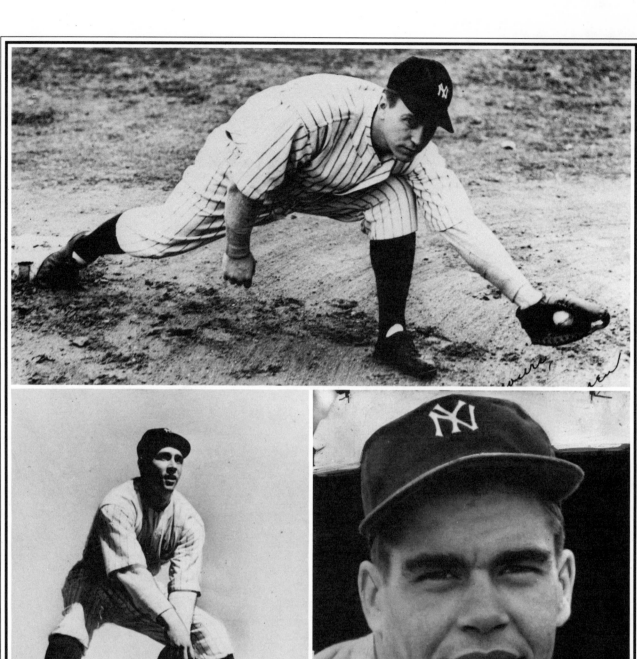

Above: Babe Dahlgren
Left: Joe Gordon
Right: Charlie Keller

Above: Mel Ott and
Carl Hubbell. *Below:*
the 1930 St. Louis Cardinals.

Clockwise from top left: Dizzy Dean;
(left) Pepper Martin;
Branch Rickey; Leo Durocher.

Branch Rickey. The previous pattern in baseball was acquisition of players by purchase or trade. Rickey innovated the farm system by obtaining players from minor league teams allied with what was known as the "parent" club.

Pepper Martin, nicknamed "the Wild Horse of the Osage," was a fierce and aggressive player. He slid into bases on his belly, fielded batted balls at third base with his chest, and engaged in all types of off-the-field pranks.

Dizzy Dean was a baseball original. Winner of 109 games in half a dozen full seasons with St. Louis, possessor of a great fastball and a highly competitive temperament, Dizzy won thirty games in 1934, the same season his brother Paul won nineteen. Tripling off Detroit pitcher Firpo Marberry in the opening game of the 1934 World Series, Dizzy Dean yelled out, "What was that you throwed me?" It was that kind of ungrammatical vocabulary and brashness that made Dean a folk hero of his time.

The Cardinals engaged in a heated rivalry with the Chicago Cubs, who won the NL pennant in 1932, 1935, and 1938 but lost in the World Series each time. Cub stars during that era included Charlie Grimm, Billy Herman, Gabby Hartnett, Phil Cavaretta, Lon Warnecke, and Stan Hack.

The Detroit Tigers, winning two pennants, supplied much of the competition during the 1930s for the Yankees. Future Hall of Famers on the Tigers included power-hitting first baseman Hank Greenberg, catcher Mickey Cochrane, second baseman Charlie Gehringer, outfielder Goose Goslin, plus standout pitchers "Schoolboy" Rowe and Tommy Bridges.

Despite the quality of its players and the brightness of its stars, major league baseball was hard hit by the Depression. Fans were still intensely interested in the game, but they just did not have money to spend on it. Attendance and gate receipts dropped sharply, forcing baseball to react and adjust in various ways.

Owners such as Philadelphia's Connie Mack sold off star players to keep their franchises in business. Mack sold superstars such as Al Simmons, Lefty Grove, Mickey Cochrane, Jimmy Foxx, and others. Teams also attempted to cut expenses by reducing the salaries of players quite a bit.

All types of promotional devices were put in place by baseball executives to make the game more commercially appealing. Special event days were scheduled; prizes and giveaways were available at ballparks. Fans were even allowed to retain baseballs that

Above: Charles "Gabby" Hartnett
and Goose Goslin. *Below:*
(right) Mickey Cochrane.

Above left:
Tommy Bridges.

Above right:
Connie Mack (left)
and John McGraw,
choosing up sides
for the first
All-Star Game.

Below: the first
night baseball
game, on
May 24, 1935.

Above: Babe Ruth and Lou Gehrig in Yankee Stadium, at a ceremony given in Gehrig's honor on July 4, 1939. Gehrig died in 1941 of a tragic disease later named for him.

Below: Bob Feller.

were hit into the stands. On May 24, 1933, the annual All-Star Game—an exhibition contest between the National and American leagues—was begun. The game did a great deal to publicize the top stars of baseball.

The first radio broadcast of a baseball game took place during the 1921 World Series. In 1947, NBC ran the first primitive telecast of a baseball game. Radio revenue and the expectation of more money from TV in the future cheered baseball owners in the 1940s.

Night baseball—another innovation to fight the Depression's drain—originated at Cincinnati's Crosley Field in May 1935. President Franklin D. Roosevelt flicked a switch and turned night into day, transforming baseball forever. Night baseball provided working people with more opportunities to attend games and thus boosted attendance.

Little League baseball began in 1939 in Williamsport, Pennsylvania. The first games—in a program that would later become the largest youth baseball organization in the world, involving over 500,000 adult volunteers operating 16,000 chartered programs in twenty-five countries—were played on a city playground.

As the sad decade of the thirties came to a close, Bob Feller of Cleveland struck out a record eighteen batters in one game, accentuating the magic, drama, and unexpected nature of baseball. The sport had endured through a decade of unemployment, bread lines, and despair. It was now poised for the years ahead.

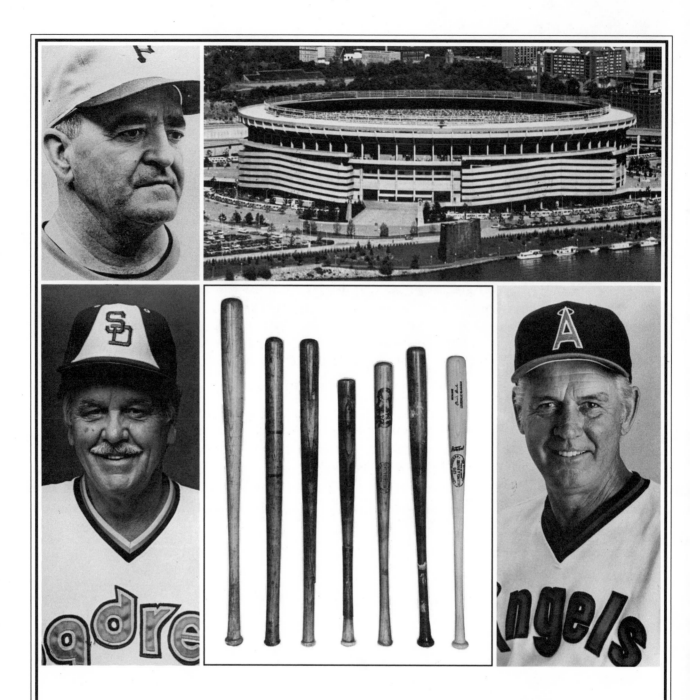

Above: top left: *Manager Danny Murtaugh of the Pittsburgh Pirates;* top right: *Three Rivers Stadium, Pittsburgh;* bottom left: *Dick Williams, manager of the San Diego Padres;* bottom right: *Manager Gene Mauch of the California Angels;* bottom center: *a display of bats including ones used by Ty Cobb (fourth from left), Babe Ruth (third from right), and Ernie Banks (far right). Opposite:* top: *Wrigley Field, home of the Chicago Cubs;* middle: *Busch Stadium, St. Louis;* bottom left: *Sparky Anderson, manager of the Detroit Tigers;* bottom center: *Manager Whitey Herzog of the St. Louis Cardinals;* bottom right: *Eddie Mathews of the Atlanta Braves.*

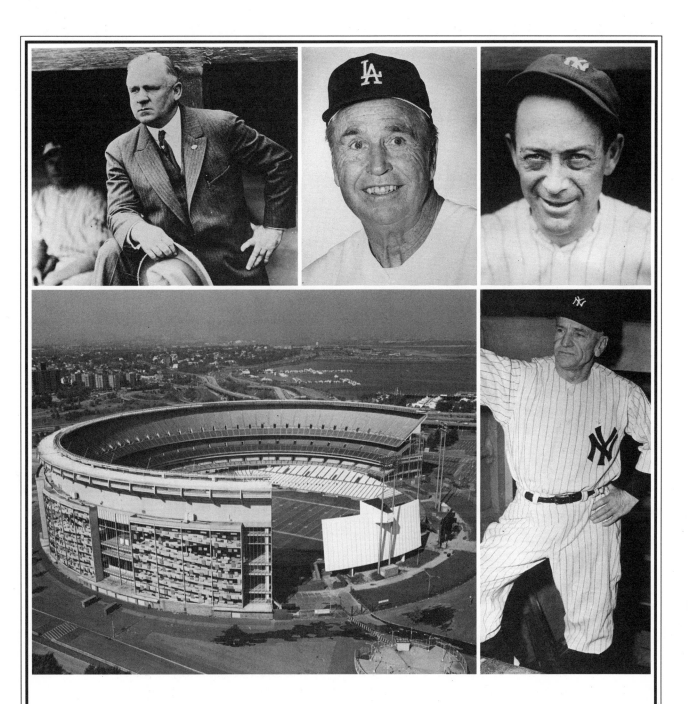

Opposite: clockwise from top left: *Yankee Stadium, home of the New York Yankees; Joe McCarthy, manager of the New York Yankees during part of the Babe Ruth era; Billy Martin, a highly publicized manager of the Yankees; Dodger Stadium in Los Angeles; Leo Durocher as a coach for the Los Angeles Dodgers; Manager Tommy Lasorda jumps for joy as his Dodgers win the 1981 World Series. Above:* top left: *John McGraw;* top center: *Walter Alston, manager of the Los Angeles Dodgers;* top right: *Miller Huggins, another manager of the New York Yankees during the Babe Ruth era;* bottom left: *Shea Stadium, home of the New York Mets;* bottom right: *Casey Stengel, manager of the New York Yankees and New York Mets.*

Chapter Five

THE WAR YEARS, INTEGRATION, AND FRANCHISE SHIFTS (1940–1959)

In 1941, the United States entered World War II, a conflict that raged until 1945 and involved the entire world in its death and destruction. Baseball was no exception. Night games were suspended as a safety precaution against airplane raids. The 1945 All-Star Game was canceled. Most teams were weakened by the manpower needs of the war, as many major leaguers became members of the U.S. armed forces. Old-timers and teenagers and players not really capable of big-league play found themselves on big-league rosters. Joe Nuxhall, exactly fifteen years, ten months, and eleven days old, pitched for Cincinnati on June 10, 1944, and became the youngest player ever to see action in a major league game.

Cincinnati, like most teams, did what it could to cope with the demands of the war. The New York Yankees, however, rolled on. The 1941 season began a twenty-four-year era of domination by the Yankees—a period in which they won eighteen pennants and twelve World Series. Yankee efficiency and power were showcased from 1941 to 1943 as the New Yorkers won three pennants and led the league in home run production. In the 1941 season Yankee centerfielder Joe DiMaggio hit safely in a record fifty-six consecutive games. His streak captured the imagination of baseball fans all over the country. "I felt a little downhearted when the streak was stopped," DiMaggio noted. "I wanted it to go on forever." That same season Ted Williams of the Boston Red Sox recorded a batting average of .406, making him the last man in baseball history to bat .400. "I was getting paid $30,000 a year," Williams joked. "The least I could do was hit .400."

Another team that prevailed through the war years was the St. Louis Cardinals. Loaded with a strong nucleus of talent from the extensive farm system developed by Branch Rickey, the Red-

Above left: Joe Nuxhall;
Right: Joe DiMaggio;
Below left: Ted Williams

Left: Stan Musial
Right: Enos Slaughter

birds finished second in the National League in 1941 and then won pennants in 1942, 1943, and 1944. In 1946, they won the pennant again and defeated the Boston Red Sox in the World Series. The Cardinals, a hustling and attractive team, featured future Hall of Famers Stan Musial, Enos Slaughter, Marty Marion, Terry Moore, Whitey Kurowski, and a host of other solid players.

April 15, 1947, was an historic day for baseball. On that day Jackie Roosevelt Robinson, a black man, played first base for the Dodgers at Ebbets Field in Brooklyn, New York, shattering baseball's age-old color line. Although Robinson, a former star athlete at UCLA, encountered many episodes of prejudice in his first few seasons, he prevailed. Winner of the Rookie of the Year award in 1947 and the Most Valuable Player award in 1949, he paved the way for black athletes to play in the major leagues: Larry Doby, Roy Campanella, Don Newcombe, Jim Gilliam, Willie Mays, Monte Irvin, and the others who followed. Robinson was also the spark that made the Dodgers a winning team. Carl Erskine, Pee Wee Reese, Duke Snider, Carl Furillo, Gil Hodges, and Roy Campanella, Don Newcombe, Jim Gilliam, and Jackie Robinson were the heart of a Dodger team that dominated the National League from 1947 to 1956, winning six pennants. In 1955, the "Bums" defeated their hated rivals, the New York Yankees, in the World Series. That Dodger victory was their first World Series win in eight attempts and the first World Series defeat for the Yankees since 1942.

The dominance of the Yankees thrilled their fans; however, it irritated supporters of other teams. From 1947 to 1957, the Yankees averaged around ninety-eight victories each season. Nine times they finished first, once second, and once third. In 1949, they won the first of a record five straight pennants. Nine of those eleven years they ranked first or second in team batting. The eccentric and shrewd Casey Stengel managed the Yankees and masterfully maximized the team's talent. He was skilled in platooning players and making the right moves in the pressure of game situations. Stengel was also an expert at double-talk. The man affectionately called the "Old Professor" managed a team whose organization had great wealth and talent. As soon as one great player retired or slowed down, there was always another one waiting to take his place. The most remarkable example of this pattern took place in 1951. Joe DiMaggio played in his final

Jackie Robinson (right) with
black baseball great Satchel Paige.

Above left: Robinson out as he slides into third. *Above right:* Don Newcombe. *Below left:* Monte Irvin. *Below right:* Roy Campanella (right) receiving the National League's MVP award of 1951.

Above: the Brooklyn Dodgers of 1951.
Below: the 1958 New York Yankees.

season in 1951, but that same year was the rookie season of Mickey Mantle, a speedy switch-hitter. Thus, the man whom many had called the best player of his generation was replaced by a man many others would call the best player of *his* generation.

Other Yankee star players of that era included pitchers Vic Raschi, Eddie Lopat, Allie Reynolds, and Whitey Ford; infielders Billy Martin, Jerry Coleman, Phil Rizzuto, and Bill Skowron; outfielders Hank Bauer and Gene Woodling; and catchers Yogi Berra and Elston Howard. The staggering amount of New York Yankee talent created both envy and animosity among other teams.

From 1947 to 1957, the only AL team to win the pennant aside from the Yankees was Cleveland. The Indians won the 1948 pennant aided by the hitting of Larry Doby, the first black player in the American League, and the superb pitching of Bob Lemon, Gene Bearden, and Bob Feller, who collectively won fifty-nine games. The Indians captured the 1954 pennant on the strength of forty-six victories from Lemon and Early Wynn, plus three other pitchers with double figure wins. Doby supplied the power, leading the league in home runs and RBIs, while infielder Bobby Avila was the AL batting champion.

In the National League, the New York Giants were the only team other than the Brooklyn Dodgers to win more than one pennant in the 1947 to 1957 era. Their 1951 pennant was the result of one of the most dramatic finishes in the history of sports. The Giants trailed the Dodgers in the NL standings by 13½ games on August 11. Managed by former Dodger pilot Leo Durocher, the Giants—with the scrappy double-play combination of Eddie Stanky and Alvin Dark, the power hitting of Monte Irvin, the steady play of Bobby Thomson and Whitey Lockman, and the clutch hitting of Larry Jansen and Sal Maglie—won thirty-seven of their last forty-four games to tie the Dodgers for first place.

"We never said we were going to win the pennant," Monte Irvin later recalled. "We said 'Let's see how close we can get.' We kept on winning, and the Dodgers kept on losing. It seemed like we beat everybody in the seventh, eighth, and ninth inning."

Going into the ninth inning of the final game of the second playoff in NL history, the Giants were trailing the Dodgers 4–1. Then Bobby Thomson hit a Ralph Branca pitch for "the shot heard 'round the world," a three-run homer tying the game and allowing the Giants to later gain an incredible 5–4 victory and

Left: Whitey Ford

Above: Yankee sluggers
(l to r) Phil Rizzuto,
Joe DiMaggio, Yogi Berra,
and Jerry Coleman.

Facing page, above:
Eddie Stanky (left)
and Sal Maglie.

Below: Bobby Thomson
touches home plate
with one of the most
exciting and memorable
game finishes in
baseball history.

the pennant. It was perhaps the most supercharged moment in all the many confrontations between the Giants of New York and the Dodgers of Brooklyn.

In 1958, fans of the Dodgers and Giants received a shock of a different nature. The Dodgers suddenly announced they were moving to Los Angeles and the Giants announced they were moving to San Francisco. Although the Dodgers had been the most prosperous major league franchise in the five seasons before they moved, their owner, Walter O'Malley, claimed his team needed a new ballpark in a better neighborhood. New York Giants owner Horace Stoneham voiced the same sentiment. When government aid was not offered, the two teams moved.

The Dodgers' and Giants' moves were just two in a series of franchise shifts during the 1950s. In 1953, the Boston Braves relocated to Milwaukee. The following year the St. Louis Browns moved their operation to Baltimore. And in 1955 the Philadelphia Athletics went to Kansas City. All these moves altered a structure that had been in place for half a century. The transfers were promoted by the teams hoping to make more money in what they perceived as more lucrative markets.

Chapter Six

THE TUMULTUOUS SIXTIES

By 1960, many cities were desirous of obtaining major league franchises. Plans were set in motion by Branch Rickey to form the Continental League—a third major league. Organized baseball responded by authorizing expansion: The Washington Senators became the Minnesota Twins in 1961, and a new franchise was supposed to be organized in Washington but never got started. Another AL expansion team (the Angels) was created in Los Angeles. In 1962, the New York Mets and Houston Astros began play in the National League as expansion franchises. In 1969, a team in Kansas City was organized to replace the Athletics, who had moved on to Oakland. A Seattle franchise was also formed but lasted only one season and then moved to Milwaukee. The National League added franchises in San Diego and in Montreal—the first major league team to be located outside the United States.

Franchise moves and expansion changed some of the organizational structure of baseball. A 162-game schedule replaced the traditional 154-game format in 1962. In 1969, because so many teams were out of the race early in the unwieldy twelve-team pennant races (causing attendance to drop), the clubs within each league were divided into Eastern and Western divisions, with a five-game championship series at the end of the season to determine the pennant winners.

Despite all the shuffling of teams and several changes in schedule, the sixties proved to be a decade of outstanding individual and team accomplishments. For example, Roger Maris, then a twenty-six-year-old New York Yankee outfielder, broke Babe Ruth's single-season record by hitting sixty-one home runs in 1961. The accomplishment was remarkable; it also stirred up much controversy, especially after Baseball Commissioner Ford

Frick ruled that Maris's feat would appear in the record books with an asterisk. Frick argued that Maris had played in a 162-game season, while Ruth had played on a 154-game schedule.

The Maris home run record was the headline accomplishment of the 1961 Yankees, a team that won the second in a string of five straight pennants. Many experts think that 1961 team was the best of the decade. The Yanks won 109 games and hammered a record 240 home runs. Maris and Mantle combined for 115 home runs, another record. Whitey Ford compiled a 25–4 mark. The Yankee lefthander also recorded his eighth straight World Series triumph as the Yanks defeated Cincinnati in five games in the Fall Classic. The triumph helped erase the bitter memory of the Yankees' 1960 World Series loss to Pittsburgh on Bill Mazeroski's seventh-game, bottom-of-the-ninth-inning home run.

The other New York City team—the Mets—also captured a share of headlines during the tumultuous sixties. Going into their eighth season as an expansion franchise, the Mets had a dismal record of 394–734. They were a hundred to one underdog to win the NL pennant in 1969. In fact, they were 9½ games out of first place on August 13 but won thirty-eight of their last forty-nine games to win the Eastern Division race in the first year of divisional play.

"We were making plays that we didn't even expect ourselves to make," recalled Met relief pitcher Tug McGraw. "We played a kind of reckless ball and it worked."

The Mets swept Atlanta in the playoffs. The Baltimore Orioles, winners of their AL division race by nineteen games, were the competition in the World Series. "We are here," Brooks Robinson of Baltimore snapped just before the World Series started, "to prove there is no Santa Claus."

But perhaps there is, because after losing the first game of the series, the Mets rallied to win four in a row. Met pitching limited Baltimore to just six runs and a .146 batting average in those games. They were called the "Miracle Mets," and stars such as pitchers Tom Seaver, Jerry Koosman, and Tug McGraw, and sluggers such as Ron Swoboda, Tommie Agee, Cleon Jones, and Donn Clendenon became national heroes.

The other highly dramatic World Series confrontation during that era took place in 1967. The Red Sox, ninth-place finishers in 1966, won the 1967 pennant on the final day of the AL sea-

Roger Maris (left)
and Mickey Mantle

Above: the 1969 New York Mets.

Left: Tom Seaver with his third Cy Young Award.

son. Their World Series competition was St. Louis. The Cardinals were a solid team that featured veteran Roger Maris, acquired from the Yankees, Orlando Cepeda, Lou Brock, Tim McCarver, and Curt Flood. Boston forced the series to a seventh game only to lose to the overpowering St. Louis righthander Bob Gibson.

One of the premier performers of the decade, Gibson was spectacular in that series, allowing just three earned runs in three complete game victories. He recorded twenty-six strikeouts and walked just five batters. Gibson compiled a remarkable string of seven straight World Series game triumphs during the sixties.

Pitchers managed to obtain their share of headlines during the 1960s despite the many exceptional hitters in major league baseball. Besides Gibson, other star hurlers of the 1960s included Juan Marichal, Sandy Koufax, Don Drysdale, and Denny McLain.

A stylish righthander for the San Francisco Giants, Marichal recorded 191 victories from 1960 to 1969, twenty-seven more than Gibson achieved during the same time frame. The left-handed Koufax and the righthanded Drysdale won 209 games in five seasons for the Los Angeles Dodgers. In 1968, Drysdale hurled six straight shutouts and fifty-eight consecutive scoreless innings. Koufax, a three-time Cy Young Award winner, won 129 games and lost just forty-seven from 1961 to 1966 and had four straight seasons in which he pitched no-hitters. McClain won thirty-one games in 1968 and led the Detroit Tigers to the pennant.

Base stealers served up a lot of excitement during the era. In 1962, Maury Wills, an infielder for the Los Angeles Dodgers, stole 104 bases, breaking the previous season record of 96 held by Ty Cobb. Wills was the premier base stealer for the first half of the decade. Then Cardinal outfielder Lou Brock took the lead in that category, ultimately shattering the mark set by Wills and setting an all-time record of 938 stolen bases.

Other outstanding 1960s individual performers included LA's Tommy Davis, a .346 average in 1962, 230 hits, 153 RBIs; Cincinnati's Pete Rose, four seasons of 200 or more hits; Pittsburgh's Roberto Clemente, four batting titles and the only player other than Rose to record 200 hits four times during the decade; Carl Yastrzemski; Tony Oliva; Frank Robinson; Ken Boyer; and Harmon Killebrew.

Above: the 1967 Boston Red Sox. *Below:* Sandy Koufax (left) and Juan Marichal.

THAT 000
BREAKS 0 0
THE 0 0
000 RECORD 0 0
0 0 --56 1-3 000
0 0 INNINGS
0 0 SCORELESS
000 PITCHING

380

Above: Maury Wills (left).
Below: Don Drysdale.

Above: Carl Yastrzemski (left) and Lou Brock. *Below:* Ken Boyer (left) and Frank Robinson. *Facing page:* Harmon Killebrew.

Chapter Seven

THE 1970s

The eighth decade of the twentieth century witnessed many exciting and memorable moments for the national pastime. Frantic pennant races, closely contested World Series, talented performers, colorful and competent teams—all were part of the picture.

Al Kaline and Brooks Robinson, two of the greatest AL players of their era, retired. Kaline, who never played minor league baseball, ended his twenty-two year career in 1974. The classy Detroit Tiger outfielder played in fifteen All-Star games, recorded 3,007 lifetime hits, and batted .300 or better nine times. Robinson, one of the all-time top fielding third basemen, was with Baltimore for twenty-three straight seasons. He set records for the most games played by a third baseman, most total chances, most assists, most double plays, and most years leading the league in fielding. He is especially remembered for his outstanding fielding plays against Cincinnati in the 1970 World Series.

Both Kaline and Robinson, unprepossessing stars who played out their entire careers for the same team, athletes who symbolized the cities they played for, were throwbacks to a more innocent time in baseball history. The decade of the 1970s was also the time of a mini-dynasty in Oakland and good times for the Cincinnati Reds, Baltimore Orioles, New York Yankees, and Pittsburgh Pirates.

The Oakland A's won five divisional titles from 1971 to 1975 and three world championships. In 1972, behind the splendid relief pitching of Rollie Fingers and the hitting of Gene Tenace, the A's defeated the Reds in seven games in the World Series. The next year Oakland, again aided greatly by the relief work of Fingers and Darrell Knowles, defeated the New York Mets in the Fall Classic. The third straight A's World Series triumph was at the expense of the Los Angeles Dodgers. A calm and collected Fingers won one game and saved three others as Oakland took the series in five games.

The Cincinnati Reds won back-to-back world championships in 1975 and 1976. The "Big Red Machine" of 1976 is regarded by many as the best team of the 1970s. Five of its players batted over .300 during the regular season. As a team the Reds in 1976 led the National League in hitting, scoring runs, and fielding. Cincinnati was loaded with stars such as Johnny Bench, Joe Morgan, Pete Rose, George Foster, and Ken Griffey.

Bench, just twenty years old when he became a Cincinnati regular in 1968, was the first catcher to be named Rookie of the Year. In 1970 and 1972, Bench won the Most Valuable Player award—a tribute to his power hitting, leadership, and exceptional defensive skills behind the plate.

Becoming the National League's youngest MVP winner in 1970, the twenty-two-year-old Bench broke long-standing records for home runs and RBIs by a catcher with league high marks of 45 and 148, respectively. He also collected his third straight Gold Glove award as he perfected the one-handed catching style that would become popular with a number of catchers in the years ahead. In 1980, the powerfully built Bench tied a record by catching a hundred or more games for the thirteenth straight year. In 1972 he led the National League in homers and RBIs and finished third in total bases. Bench's performance was one of the reasons the 1972 Reds won their second NL pennant in three years.

Another big part of the Cincinnati success story was Pete Rose. The first singles hitter to earn $100,000, the National League's 1973 MVP, the 1975 World Series MVP, the NL Player of the Decade of the 1970s (named by *Sporting News* and *Baseball Magazine*), Pete Rose was the piston that fired the "Big Red Machine." Dubbed "Charley Hustle" because of his all-out style of play, Rose personified dedication and drive. On August 5, 1979, he recorded his 2,427th single, becoming the all-time best singles hitter in the history of the National League. That 1979 season Rose, along with Lou Brock and Carl Yastrzemski, became members of the exclusive 3,000-hits-in-a-career club. The 1970s were indeed a busy time for that record-setting feat, as seven players, including Willie Mays and Hank Aaron, reached or surpassed that magic mark.

Above: Rollie Fingers (left)
and Willie Mays.
Below: the 1976 Cincinnati Reds.
Facing page, above:
Pete Rose (left).
Below: Johnny Bench.

Baltimore's Orioles won the first World Series of the decade and had a chance in 1971 for two in a row, but they lost to the Pirates. Baltimore was a team that was deep in pitching. Stylish Jim Palmer, their best hurler of the period, teamed with Dave McNally and Mike Cuellar for a collective 188 wins and 2.89 ERA from 1969 to 1977. Seven times a twenty-game winner in the 1970s, Palmer was also a three-time Cy Young award winner. The Orioles again faced the Pirates in the 1979 World Series and achieved the same losing results. Pittsburgh, playing with the song "We Are Family" as their theme to unite the team and the city, battered Oriole pitching. Five Pirates racked up ten or more hits in the series, and Willie Stargell rapped out a record seven extra base hits.

Built by trades, the signing of free agents, and some products from their farm system, the New York Yankees were one of the most flamboyant franchises of the 1970s. Yankee stars included sluggers Reggie Jackson and Thurman Munson; starting pitchers Catfish Hunter and Ron Guidry; and relief pitchers Goose Gossage and Sparky Lyle. Swept by the Cincinnati Reds in the 1976 World Series, the Yankees came back to defeat the Los Angeles Dodgers in 1977 and 1978.

Reggie Jackson, dubbed "Mr. October" because of his dramatic play in that month, hammered five home runs in the 1977 World Series. Three of the home runs came in Game Six, on Jackson's first swing in three consecutive at bats. In 1978, the Yankees lost the first two games of the series but swept the next four as Jackson, and the usually weak-hitting Bucky Dent and Brian Doyle, drove in half the New York runs.

Two of the most outstanding individual feats of the 1970s were accomplished by Hank Aaron and Lou Brock. In 1973, Aaron played in his twentieth season as a major leaguer. By season's end, he had recorded forty home runs for the year. He needed one more home run to tie and two to break the magic number of 714 lifetime home runs set by Babe Ruth.

During the winter, Aaron thought a great deal about the record and about Babe Ruth. "He'll still be the best," Aaron said, "even if I pass him. The Babe will still be regarded as the greatest home run hitter that ever lived."

On April 4 in Cincinnati, on the first day of the 1974 season, Hank Aaron came to bat for Atlanta in the first inning. There were two men on base. On his first swing of the season, Aaron

Above: Jim Palmer (left) and Willie Stargell (right). Stargell displays his Lou Gehrig Award for 1974.

Left: Sparky Lyle.

Reggie Jackson

Henry Aaron

smashed number 714, and the thirty-nine-year-old record of Babe Ruth was tied. On April 8, at Atlanta Stadium before a crowd of more than 53,000 and a national television audience, Aaron achieved his goal of becoming the all-time career leader in home runs.

Aaron walked in the first inning. In the fourth inning, in his second at bat against Al Downing of the Los Angeles Dodgers, he took his first swing. The ball streaked toward left centerfield and dropped over the fence. Henry Louis Aaron now stood alone in history with home run number 715.

The talented athlete who was affectionately nicknamed Bad Henry would play on through the 1974 season and then on a part-time basis the next two years. He would complete his outstanding twenty-three-year career with a grand total of 755 home runs.

In 1971, St. Louis outfielder Lou Brock became the first player in history to steal fifty or more bases in seven straight seasons. His career stolen base record then stood at 501. In 1975, Brock leaped from ninth on the all-time stolen base list to second place when he stole 118 bases to shatter Maury Wills's single-season stolen base mark.

On August 29, 1977, the thirty-eight-year-old Brock did some knee bends and walked out onto the field at San Diego Stadium. He needed just one stolen base to tie and another to break Ty Cobb's legendary mark of 892.

Leading off the game for the Cardinals, Brock drew a walk. On the next pitch, he took off for second base and stole it. He had tied Cobb's all-time record. In the seventh inning, Brock stole second base again—his twenty-eighth steal of the year and the 893rd of his career, one more than Ty Cobb. The game was halted, and in a brief ceremony second base was taken up and presented to Brock.

Ty Cobb's career stolen base mark was regarded as the official modern record, but "Sliding Billy" Hamilton, a turn-of-the-century performer, was in the books with 937 steals. On September 23, 1979, in his nineteenth major league season, forty-year-old Lou Brock stole number 938 to pass Sliding Billy and all the other base stealers in baseball history. A month before Brock had recorded his 3,000th hit.

"The records," Brock pointed out, "were made for immortality, and that was part of my going for them the way I did."

Two unexpected deaths of baseball superstars saddened the world of baseball during the 1970s. Both players were leaders of their teams; both died in tragic airplane crashes.

Roberto Clemente of the Pittsburgh Pirates won four batting titles in his eighteen NL seasons and compiled a lifetime batting average of .317. A fine defensive outfielder, Clemente quietly did the job. On September 30, 1972, he rapped out the 3,000th hit of his career, becoming only the eleventh player in baseball history to reach that fabled figure. As it turned out, that hit would be his last one. On New Year's Eve in 1972, Clemente was bringing food and supplies to earthquake victims in Managua, Nicaragua, when his plane crashed at sea. His body was never recovered. In 1973, a special election admitted Clemente to baseball's Hall of Fame.

Thurman Munson of the New York Yankees was one of the top catchers in all of baseball during the 1970s. A disciplined defensive player who three times won the Gold Glove award, Munson was an exceptional clutch hitter. He batted .357 in thirty postseason games. On August 2, 1979, his brilliant eleven-year career came to a shocking end when his twin-engine jet crash-landed after clipping a tree and he was killed.

Baseball's "reserve clause" system historically bound a player to a team, though owners could sell or trade athletes as they wished. In 1972, St. Louis Cardinal outfielder Curt Flood balked at a trade and took his case, unsuccessfully, to the U.S. Supreme Court. Then, in 1973, the reserve clause was modified slightly to give ten-year major league veterans the right to agree on a trade to another team. In 1976, a court ruling declared that a player could sign with any team he wished after playing out his reserve year. That ruling created the current "free agent" bidding wars.

In 1973 the American League added a controversial new rule. Called the designated hitter (DH) rule, it allowed another player to bat in place of the pitcher in the lineup. Still controversial and still not used by the National League, the rule has lengthened the careers of some hitters and made it easier for managers to decide what to do in certain clutch situations.

In 1977, the American League expanded to fourteen teams by adding franchises in Toronto and Seattle.

Six times during the 1970s, Rod Carew won the AL batting title. In 1977, the slender Panamanian had his season of sea-

Left: Thurman Munson.
Above right: Roberto Clemente.
Below: Rod Carew.

sons. He batted .400 or better for most of the year and finished with a league-leading .388 average—the highest in baseball in two decades. Carew also led the American League in 1977 in most hits, most runs scored, and most triples. These glittering statistics were more than enough to make him the American League's MVP that year. A throwback to players such as Wee Willie Keeler, Carew personified style and skilled bat control. His 1970s batting average was a gaudy .343. An injury in 1984 contributed to snapping Carew's string of fifteen straight .300 or better seasons; in 1985 his brilliant career came to an end when he retired.

Chapter Eight

THE 1980s

The 1980s brought new excitement to baseball. Varied and talented new players took their place alongside established standout players. And there were different teams virtually every season in the World Series.

In 1980, Kansas City finally defeated the New York Yankees in the AL playoffs. The Royals had lost three previous playoffs to the Yankees. The centerpiece player on the 1980 Royals was third baseman George Brett. Throughout the season he launched a spirited drive to become the first .400 hitter in baseball since Ted Williams accomplished that feat in 1941. Brett fell just a bit short of the mark and finished his Most Valuable Player season with a .390 average. Willie Wilson was another contributor to the Kansas City attack. The speedy outfielder scored the most runs (133) and stroked the most hits (230) in the American League. Wilson also stole seventy-nine bases—making him runnerup to Rickey Henderson of Oakland, who stole a then-AL record one hundred bases.

Philadelphia was the competition for the Royals in the World Series. The Phillies were led by slugger Mike Schmidt, the National League's MVP, and pitcher Steve Carlton, who posted a 24–9 record in 1980 while winning his third Cy Young award. The favored Royals entered the World Series with a .268 team batting average, the highest of any team since 1950. However, Philadelphia stopped the Royals in six games to win the world championship.

In 1981, a players' strike resulted in a loss of 712 games from the major league schedule and a "split" season. The teams that led their divisions when the first half of the season ended (when play was suspended due to the strike) faced the second-half winners in a playoff that preceded the regular playoffs. The New

George Brett (right)
with Hal McRae.

Clockwise from top left:
Willie Wilson; Rickey
Henderson; Dodger
pitching sensation
Fernando Valenzuela;
and Mike Schmidt.

York Yankees and the Los Angeles Dodgers emerged victorious out of all the playoff scrambles and met in the World Series. After losing the first two games, the Dodgers won four in a row and became the 1981 world champions. Two of the more outstanding individual performers of 1981 were Mike Schmidt and Rollie Fingers. Schmidt, the Philadelphia slugger, became only the third National Leaguer to win the MVP award two years in a row. The Milwaukee relief pitcher, Fingers, saved twenty-eight games, posted a glittering earned run average of 1.04, and won the MVP award, the Cy Young award, and the Fireman of the Year award.

In 1982, the St. Louis Cardinals won their first pennant in fourteen years behind the relief pitching of Bruce Sutter, the defensive skills of shortstop Ozzie Smith, and the clutch hitting and superb fielding of first baseman Keith Hernandez. The Redbirds went on to defeat Milwaukee in the World Series. That season Pete Rose became only the fifth player in history to appear in more than 3,000 games. Gaylord Perry kept pitching, winning his three hundredth game. Rickey Henderson kept running, stealing a record 130 bases.

Many banner headlines and record achievements marked the 1983 season. Slugger Dale Murphy of Atlanta won his second straight MVP award. For a record third straight season, Rickey Henderson stole a hundred or more bases. Both Steve Carlton and Nolan Ryan passed the fabled career mark of 3,508 strikeouts set by the legendary Walter Johnson. Boston's Carl Yastrzemski became the all-time leader in games played. That 1983 season was also the last hurrah for Yastrzemski, Johnny Bench, and Gaylord Perry, three determined and outstanding players. The fiftieth anniversary All-Star game was won by the American League—its first victory after eleven straight losses to the National League. In the World Series the Philadelphia Phillies matched up against the Baltimore Orioles. The Phillies, a team that featured veteran stars Pete Rose, Joe Morgan, Mike Schmidt, and Steve Carlton, won the first game of the series, but then were swept in the next four by the talent-laden Orioles.

The 1984 baseball season gave hope to fans of many losing clubs, especially those rooting for the Chicago Cubs, the San Diego Padres, and the New York Mets. Going into the '84 season the Cubs had not won a championship of any kind in thirty-nine years. The Padres had existed for fifteen seasons and had

Ozzie Smith
(in the air)

Above: Dale Murphy (left) and
Nolan Ryan. *Below:* Steve Carlton.

never finished higher than fourth place in the standings. Improbably, these two teams faced each other in the NL championship series of 1984. San Diego prevailed over a talented Cub team that leaped from twenty games under .500 in 1983 to thirty-one games above .500 in 1984.

The Tigers of Detroit, who racked up a 35–5 mark early in the '84 season and remained in first place day in and day out throughout the year, defeated the Padres in the World Series. Tiger pilot Sparky Anderson became the first manager to win the world championship in both leagues.

The New York Mets, another losing franchise, were transformed into a contender in 1984. Led by Keith Hernandez, acquired in a trade with the St. Louis Cardinals, the Mets leaped from a sixth-place finish in 1983 to a ninety-win, second-place finish.

Keith Hernandez finished second to Chicago's Ryne Sandberg in the National League's MVP voting, but another Hernandez, Willie, won the American League's MVP award in '84. The Tiger relief pitcher saved thirty-two games and played a key role in Detroit's pennant romp.

Other impressive performers of 1984 included relief pitcher Dan Quisenberry of Kansas City, who saved forty-four games, one less than his record-setting mark of the year before; and Tony Gwynn of San Diego, whose .351 batting average easily earned him the NL title.

It wasn't that easy for Don Mattingly of the New York Yankees to win the AL batting title. All season long he battled teammate Dave Winfield for the lead. On the final day of the season Mattingly settled matters. He rapped out four hits in five at bats, finishing the year with a .343 average to Winfield's .340.

The St. Louis Cardinals and New York Mets battled each other all season long in 1985 in one of the most exciting NL pennant races in years. The Mets, strengthened by the acquisition of catcher Gary Carter, obtained in a multiple-player deal with Montreal, won ninety-eight games. Pitcher Dwight Gooden of the Mets led the league with a glittering 24–4 record, most innings pitched, and best ERA.

But the Mets finished in second place for the second straight year, as the Cardinals won the pennant with 101 victories. The Redbirds recorded the league's top batting and fielding averages and the most stolen bases. Their centerfielder Willie McGee batted

Above: Don Mattingly
(left) and Dave Winfield.
Left: Ryne Sandberg.

Left: Keith Hernandez.
Above right: Dwight Gooden.
Below right: Gary Carter.
Facing page: Willie
McGee (right).

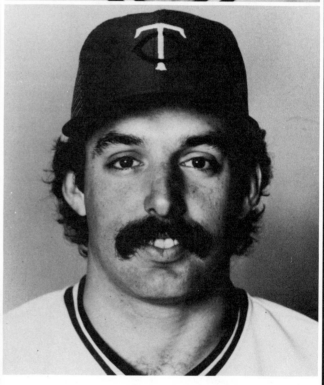

Clockwise from top left: Jack Clark; Frank Viola; Gary Gaetti; and Darryl Strawberry.

a league-leading .353 and won the MVP award. Pitchers John Tudor and Joaquin Andujar won twenty-one games each for the slick fielding, timely hitting St. Louis swifties, who defeated Los Angeles in the championship series on Jack Clark's dramatic sixth-game, ninth-inning, three-run homer.

Kansas City defeated Toronto in the AL championship series, setting up the first "I-70" World Series in history—an all-Missouri affair. The underdog Royals lost the first two games and then rebounded to win their first world championship, though it was clouded by a disputed umpire's call at first base in the sixth game and capped by an 11–0 pounding of the Cardinals in the seventh game.

The 1986 Cardinals, racked by injuries and the memory of their stunning 1985 loss to the Royals in the World Series, were never a factor in the 1986 NL East pennant race. Few teams were. The exciting Mets, featuring a superb pitching staff of Dwight Gooden, Bob Ojeda, and others, the power hitting of Darryl Strawberry, Ray Knight, and Gary Carter, the leadership of Keith Hernandez, and a very deep bench won the third pennant in their twenty-five-year history. A hard-fought Met league championship series triumph over Houston, also celebrating its silver anniversary, set up a Boston Red Sox–Mets World Series.

The Mets, like KC the year before, lost the first two games of the series. However, timely hitting and great pitching—the hallmark of the Mets all season long—enabled the New Yorkers to prevail over the powerful team from Boston in seven games. The sixth game was the most exciting of the hard-fought series, as the apparently doomed Mets were down by three runs in the ninth inning with two men out and nobody on base. Gary Carter began the rally to tie the game, which was won in the tenth inning by the Mets.

In the 1987 season, the Minnesota Twins beat the Detroit Tigers in the AL playoffs in five games, and the National League's St. Louis Cardinals beat the San Francisco Giants in seven games. The Twins went on to defeat the Cardinals in the World Series in seven games, with pitcher Frank Viola and slugger Gary Gaetti leading the way for the Twins.

Momentous accomplishments, storied stars, frantic pennant races, and thrilling World Series—all these have been a part of baseball's first 150 years. Today the sport is poised for the future and will no doubt continue to build on its exciting past.

APPENDIX

CITIES HOLDING FRANCHISES
IN THE NATIONAL LEAGUE

Atlanta	1966 to date
Boston	1876 to 1952
Brooklyn	1890 to 1957
Chicago	1876 to date
Cincinnati	1876 to 1880; 1890 to date
Houston	1962 to date
Los Angeles	1958 to date
Milwaukee	1878; 1953 to 1965
Montreal	1969 to date
New York (Giants)	1876; 1883 to 1957
New York (Mets)	1962 to date
Philadelphia	1876; 1883 to date
Pittsburgh	1887 to date
St. Louis	1876 to 1877; 1885 to 1886; 1892 to date
San Diego	1969 to date
San Francisco	1958 to date

CITIES HOLDING FRANCHISES
IN THE AMERICAN LEAGUE

Baltimore	1901–1902; 1954 to date
Boston	1901 to date
California	1961 to date
Chicago	1901 to date
Cleveland	1901 to date
Detroit	1901 to date
Kansas City	1955 to 1967; 1969 to date
Milwaukee	1901–1902; 1970 to date
Minnesota	1961 to date
New York	1903 to date
Oakland	1968 to date
Philadelphia	1901 to 1954
St. Louis (Browns)	1902 to 1953
Seattle	1969; 1977 to date
Texas	1972 to date
Toronto	1977 to date
Washington	1901 to 1960; 1961 to 1971

BASEBALL HALL OF FAME MEMBERS
199 members as of March 1988

Aaron, Henry L. "Hank" (1982)
Alexander, Grover Cleveland (1938)
Alston, Walter E. (1983)
Anson, Adrian C. "Cap" (1939)
Aparicio, Luis (1984)
Appling, Lucius B. "Luke" (1964)
Averill, H. Earl (1975)

Baker, J. Franklin "Home Run" (1955)
Bancroft, David J. (1971)
Banks, Ernest (1977)
Barrow, Edward G. (1953)
Beckley, Jacob P. (1971)
Bell, James T. "Cool Papa" (1974)
Bender, Charles A. "Chief" (1953)
Berra, Lawrence P. "Yogi" (1972)
Bottomley, James L. (1974)
Boudreau, Louis (1970)
Bresnahan, Roger P. (1945)
Brock, Lou (1985)
Brouthers, Dennis "Dan" (1945)
Brown, Mordecai P. (1949)
Bulkeley, Morgan G. (1937)
Burkett, Jesse C. (1946)

Campanella, Roy (1969)
Carey, Max G. (1961)
Cartwright, Alexander J., Jr. (1938)
Chadwick, Henry (1938)
Chance, Frank L. (1946)
Chandler, Albert B. "Happy" (1982)
Charleston, Oscar M. (1976)
Chesbro, John D. (1946)
Clarke, Frederick C. (1945)
Clarkson, John G. (1963)
Clemente, Roberto W. (1973)
Cobb, Tyrus R. (1936)
Cochrane, Gordon S. "Mickey" (1947)
Collins, Edward T. (1939)
Collins, James J. (1945)
Combs, Earle B. (1970)
Comiskey, Charles A. (1939)
Conlan, John B. "Jocko" (1974)
Connolly, Thomas H. (1953)
Connor, Roger (1976)
Coveleski, Stanley A. (1969)
Crawford, Samuel E. (1957)
Cronin, Joseph H. (1956)
Cummings, William A. "Candy" (1939)
Cuyler, Hazen S. "Kiki" (1968)

Dean, Jay H. "Dizzy" (1953)
Delahanty, Edward J. (1945)
Dickey, William M. (1954)
Dihigo, Martin (1977)
DiMaggio, Joseph P. (1955)
Doerr, Robert (1986)

Drysdale, Don (1984)
Duffy, Hugh (1945)

Evans, William G. (1973)
Evers, John J. (1946)
Ewing, William B. "Buck" (1939)

Faber, Urban C. "Red" (1964)
Feller, Robert W. A. (1962)
Ferrell, Rick (1984)
Flick, Elmer H. (1963)
Ford, Edward C. "Whitey" (1974)
Foster, Andrew "Rube" (1981)
Foxx, James E. (1951)
Frick, Ford C. (1970)
Frisch, Frank F. (1947)

Galvin, James F. "Pud" (1965)
Gehrig, H. Louis (1939)
Gehringer, Charles L. (1949)
Gibson, Joshua (1972)
Gibson, Robert (1981)
Giles, Warren C. (1979)
Gomez, Vernon L. "Lefty" (1972)
Goslin, Leon A. "Goose" (1968)
Greenberg, Henry B. (1956)
Griffith, Clark C. (1946)
Grimes, Burleigh A. (1964)
Grove, Robert M. "Lefty" (1947)

Hafey, Charles J. "Chick" (1971)
Haines, Jesse J. "Pop" (1970)
Hamilton, William R. (1961)
Harridge, William (1972)
Harris, Stanley R. "Bucky" (1975)
Hartnett, Charles L. "Gabby" (1955)
Heilmann, Harry E. (1952)
Herman, William J. (1975)
Hooper, Harry B. (1971)
Hornsby, Rogers (1942)
Hoyt, Waite C. (1969)
Hubbard, R. Cal (1976)
Hubbell, Carl O. (1947)
Huggins, Miller J. (1964)
Hunter, Jim "Catfish" (1987)

Irvin, Monford "Monte" (1973)

Jackson, Travis C. "Stonewall" (1982)
Jennings, Hugh A. (1945)
Johnson, Byron B. (1937)
Johnson, Walter P. (1936)
Johnson, William J. "Judy" (1975)
Joss, Adrian (1978)

Kaline, Albert W. (1980)
Keefe, Timothy J. (1964)

Keeler, William H. "Willie" (1939)
Kell, George C. (1983)
Kelley, Joseph J. (1971)
Kelly, George L. (1973)
Kelly, Michael J. "King" (1945)
Killebrew, Harmon (1984)
Kiner, Ralph (1975)
Klein, Charles H. (1980)
Klem, William J. (1953)
Koufax, Sanford (1972)

LaJoie, Napoleon "Larry" (1937)
Landis, Kenesaw M. (1944)
Lemon, Robert G. (1976)
Leonard, Walter F. "Buck" (1972)
Lindstrom, Frederick C. (1976)
Lloyd, John H. (1977)
Lombardi, Ernest (1986)
Lopez, Alfonso R. (1977)
Lyons, Theodore A. (1955)

Mack, Connie (1937)
MacPhail, Leland S. "Larry" (1978)
Mantle, Mickey C. (1974)
Manush, Henry E. "Heinie" (1964)
Maranville, Walter J. "Rabbit" (1954)
Marichal, Juan A. (1983)
Marquard, Richard W. "Rube" (1971)
Mathews, Edwin L. (1978)
Mathewson, Christopher (1936)
Mays, Willie H. (1979)
McCarthy, Joseph V. (1957)
McCarthy, Thomas F. (1946)
McCovey, William (1986)
McGinnity, Joseph J. "Iron Man" (1946)
McGraw, John J. (1937)
McKechnie, William B. (1962)
Medwick, Joseph M. (1968)
Mize, John R. (1981)
Musial, Stanley F. (1969)

Nichols, Charles A. "Kid" (1949)

O'Rourke, James H. (1945)
Ott, Melvin T. (1951)

Paige, Leroy R. "Satchel" (1971)
Pennock, Herbert J. (1948)
Plank, Edward S. (1946)

Radbourne, Charles G. (1939)
Reese, Pee Wee (1984)
Rice, Edgar C. "Sam" (1963)

Rickey, W. Branch (1967)
Rixey, Eppa (1963)
Roberts, Robin E. (1976)
Robinson, Brooks C. (1983)
Robinson, Frank (1982)
Robinson, Jack R. (1962)
Robinson, Wilbert (1945)
Roush, Edd J. (1962)
Ruffing, Charles H. "Red" (1967)
Rusie, Amos W. (1977)
Ruth, George H. "Babe" (1936)

Schalk, Raymond W. (1955)
Sewell, Joseph H. (1977)
Simmons, Aloysius H. (1953)
Sisler, George H. (1939)
Slaughter, Enos (1985)
Snider, Edwin D. "Duke" (1980)
Spahn, Warren E. (1973)
Spalding, Albert G. (1939)
Speaker, Tristram E. (1937)
Stargell, William (1988)
Stengel, Charles D. "Casey" (1966)

Terry, William H. (1954)
Thompson, Samuel L. (1974)
Tinker, Joseph B. (1946)
Traynor, Harold J. "Pie" (1948)

Vance, Arthur C. "Dazzy" (1955)
Vaughan, Arky (1985)

Waddell, George E. "Rube" (1946)
Wagner, John P. "Honus" (1936)
Wallace, Roderick J. "Bobby" (1953)
Walsh, Edward A. (1946)
Waner, Lloyd J. (1967)
Waner, Paul G. (1952)
Ward, John M. (1964)
Weiss, George M. (1971)
Welch, Michael F. (1973)
Wheat, Zachariah D. (1959)
Wilhelm, Hoyt (1985)
Williams, Billy (1987)
Williams, Theodore S. (1966)
Wilson, Lewis R. "Hack" (1979)
Wright, George (1937)
Wright, William H. "Harry" (1953)
Wynn, Early (1972)

Yawkey, Thomas A. (1980)
Young, Denton T. "Cy" (1937)
Youngs, Ross M. (1972)

INDEX